INTRODUCTION

In this book, you will find 50 mazes featuring **Dinosaurs and other creatures** from the prehistoric era. Part of the fun of the book is not just solving the mazes but learning about prehistoric creatures and the eras in which they lived.

The mazes have been given difficulty levels from 1 to 5. You can start with a level 1 and work your way up to 5, or feel free to solve the mazes randomly. The difficulty level is determined by how long it should take to solve the maze. A level 5 maze might be perfect for the car ride to Grandma's house, but a quick level 1 might be just right before bedtime.

Mazes start at the start and finish at the finish—doesn't that make sense? But it's not quite that simple. Sometimes there are multiple paths leading out from the **START** and most of the **FINISH** points have several paths leading out as well (for those sneaky kids who like to start from the finish!).

Choose your paths wisely. Take your time. Try not to get frustrated. If you get stumped on a maze, take a break and come back to it later. If you get really, really stumped, the solutions are in the back of the book, but try not to peek!

GOOD LUCK and have some **Prehistoric** fun!

B.E.S.
PUBLISHING

Solutions

Page 2

Page 3

Page 4

Page 5

Page 6

Page 7

Page 8

Page 9

Page 10

Page 11

Page 12

Page 13

Page 14

Page 15

Page 16

Page 17

Page 18

Page 19

Page 20

Page 21

Page 22

Page 23

Page 24

Page 25

Page 26

Page 27

Page 28

Page 29

Page 30

Page 31

Page 32

Page 33

Solutions

Page 34

Page 35

Page 36

Page 37

Page 38

Page 39

Page 40

Page 41

Page 42

Page 43

Page 44

Page 45

Page 46

Page 47

Page 48

Page 49

Page 50

Page 51

© Copyright 2018 by Joe Wos
Illustrations © copyright 2018 by Joe Wos
Cover design © copyright 2018 by Joe Wos

All rights reserved.
No part of this publication may be reproduced or
distributed in any form or by any means without the
written permission of the copyright owner.

All inquiries should be addressed to:
B.E.S. Publishing
250 Wireless Boulevard
Hauppauge, NY 11788
www.bes-publishing.com

ISBN: 978-1-4380-1227-8

Date of Manufacture: February 2019
Manufactured by: WKT, Shenzhen, China

Printed in China
9 8 7 6 5 4 3 2